ANIMALES
ANIMALS

This book provides bilingual materials to teach a fun and comprehensive unit about ANIMALS. Included is a teacher's instruction section with details for each project along with ideas to use throughout the classroom. Discover ANIMALS using skills in reading, math, and spelling. Both Spanish and English versions of each project are included in one book!

Cover Photos:
© 2002 Brand X Pictures
© Photodisc

ISBN 1-59441-639-7

Dear Family Letter (pages 6–7)

Dear Family,

We are starting a unit about ANIMALS. We will learn about many different kinds of animals including pets, sea animals, zoo animals, and farm animals.

Please join us by including daily conversations about animals at home. Be sure to include any experiences you have had with animals in your discussions. Family discussions will help reinforce the concepts we are learning in class.

When visiting the public library, look for books about animals with your child. Thank you for helping your child learn more about animals!

Sincerely,

Send this note home with students to let families know what is happening in the classroom. The letter introduces families to the upcoming unit about animals.

Animals Certificates (pages 8–9)

This is a great way to recognize and reward students as they progress through this unit about ANIMALS.

Use the Animals Certificates as incentives when students finish a defined list of projects or as general awards when the unit is complete. The certificates make a great classroom bulletin board display and provide students with take-home diplomas that they can be proud of.

ANIMALS

CERTIFICATE

Name:____________________

Congratulations! You are now an expert on animals!

I know about ANIMALS!

Copy the certificates onto colorful paper or let students color their own certificates as a classroom art project.

Animal Cards (pages 10–15)

The animal cards included in this book can be used in a variety of creative ways to make learning with flash cards fun and interesting.

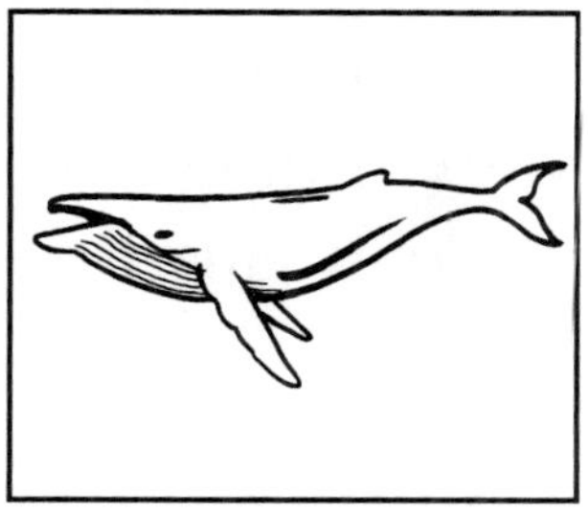

Flash Cards

Make different flash card decks of varying degrees of difficulty to use as assessment tools. Display transparencies of the cards for reference during classroom discussions.

Assembly Instructions

Copy the desired word cards onto colorful, sturdy paper and cut out. Copy the English cards on one side and copy the Spanish cards on the other side. Or, copy the picture cards on one side and the English or Spanish word cards on the other side. Laminate cards for permanent use in the classroom and/or make sets for each student to use at home.

Concentration

This ever-popular game helps students develop memory and matching skills. Concentration works best when played in small groups.

There are several variations of "Animal Concentration." Increase difficulty by mixing and matching combinations. For example, students can match animal picture cards to animal word cards.

Assembly Instructions

Copy the desired animal cards onto sturdy paper and cut them out. Laminate cards for permanent use.

How to Play

1. Mix up the cards and place them facedown in rows.
2. Have students take turns choosing two cards at a time. If a student chooses two cards that match, she takes another turn. If there is no match, she turns the cards facedown, and the next player takes a turn. The player with the most matched pairs wins the game!

Animal Mobiles (pages 16–25)

This fun art project reinforces the skills and vocabulary learned in the ANIMALS unit. Use it as a classroom decoration or to identify centers that focus on specific types of animals.

Assembly Instructions

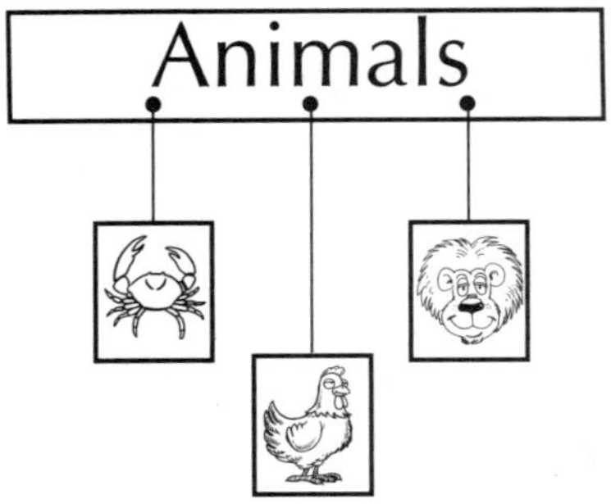

Select a "header card" and the desired animal cards for a mobile and copy onto sturdy paper. Use the animal picture or word cards (pages 10–15) or use the mobile cards that include the names and pictures of the animals. Provide crayons, paint, or markers and have students color their mobile pieces. After coloring, have students fold the header cards and punch holes as indicated. Let students tape string, yarn, fishing line, or dental floss to the backs of the word cards. Then, have students glue the coordinating picture card to the back of each word card. When the glue dries, let students tie the animal cards to the header cards. Hang the mobiles from the ceiling or in a window.

Venn Diagrams (pages 26–29)

This book includes essential Venn diagram reproducibles. Use them as transparencies to aid in classroom discussions or give one copy to each student to complete. This is an excellent project to teach the differences and similarities between animals and to assess students' listening and comprehension skills.

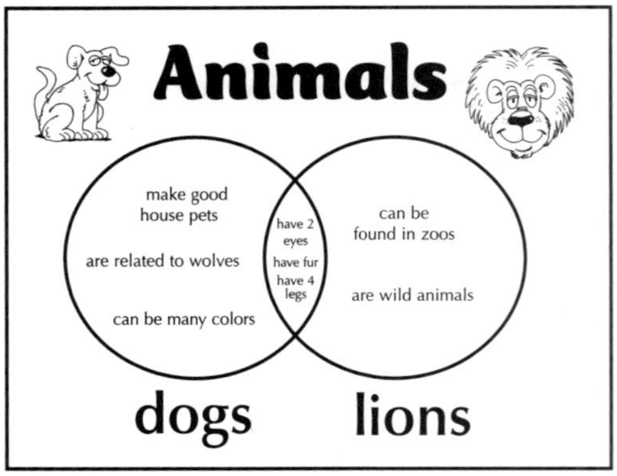

My Animal Books (pages 30–45)

Students can create and color their own books about animals. Teachers can design the books to complement a theme by choosing various pages.

Assembly Instructions

Copy one book for each student. Copy cover pages onto sturdy paper and copy inside pages onto 8½" x 11" (21.5 cm x 28 cm) white paper. Fold, assemble, and bind books using brass fasteners or staples.

Students can write stories or facts about different animals in their animal books. Have students share their finished books with the class.

These books make great take-home projects. Have students complete several books to create their own "My Animals" libraries! Finished books also make an excellent bulletin board display.

Estimada familia,

Estamos comenzando una unidad sobre los animales. Aprenderemos mucho acerca de los animales.

Por favor únanse a nosotros e incluyan conversaciones en casa acerca de los animales, a diario. Incluyan en sus pláticas experiencias que hayan tenido con los animales. Las conversaciones familiares ayudan a reforzar conceptos que se estudian en clase.

Cuando visiten la biblioteca pública, ayuden a sus hijos a buscar libros informativos acerca de los animales. Gracias por ayudar a sus hijos a aprender más sobre los animales.

Atentamente,

Dear Family,

We are starting a unit about ANIMALS. We will learn about many different kinds of animals including pets, sea animals, zoo animals, and farm animals.

Please join us by including daily conversations about animals at home. Be sure to include any experiences you have had with animals in your discussions. Family discussions will help reinforce the concepts we are learning in class.

When visiting the public library, look for books about animals with your child. Thank you for helping your child learn more about animals!

Sincerely,

ANIMALES

CERTIFICADO

Nombre:______________________________

¡Felicidades!
Ya eres un experto
sobre los animales!

ANIMALS

CERTIFICATE

Name:______________________________

Congratulations!
You are now an
expert on animals!

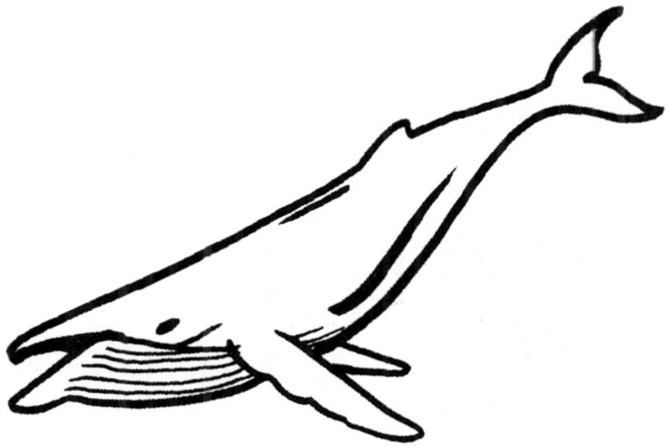

vaca	pájaro
gallina	perro
caballo	gato

bird	cow
dog	chicken
cat	horse

cangrejo	elefante
ballena	mono
foca	león

elephant	crab
monkey	whale
lion	seal

Móviles de los animales

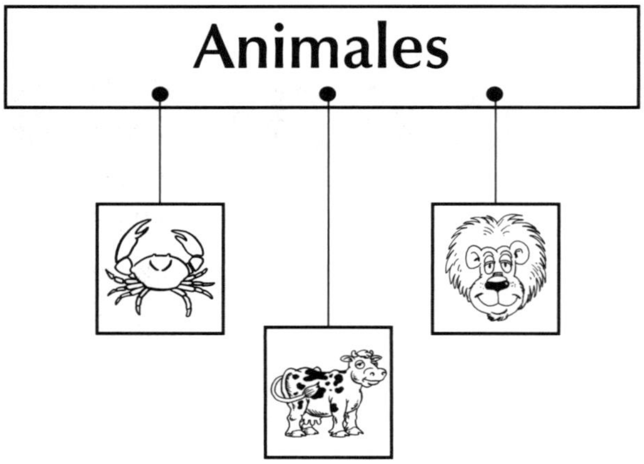

Animales

Animales

Animal Mobiles

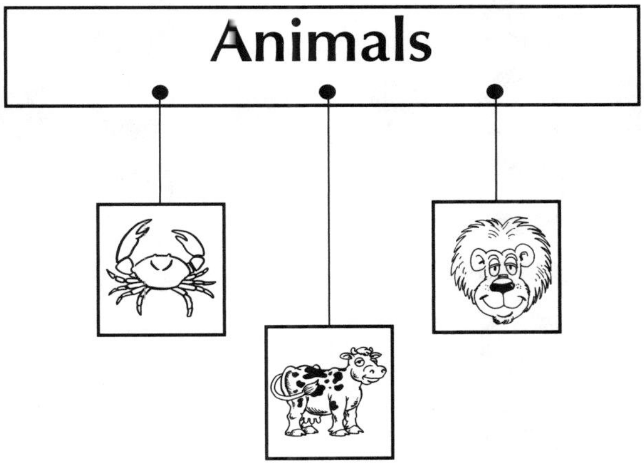

Animals

Animals

Animales Marinos

Animales Marinos

Mascotas

Mascotas

Pets

Pets

Sea Animals

Sea Animals

Animales de la granja

Animales de la granja

Animales del zoológico

Animales del zoológico

Zoo Animals

Zoo Animals

Farm Animals

Farm Animals

pájaro

vaca

perro

gallina

gato

caballo

cow

bird

chicken

dog

horse

cat

elefante

cangrejo

mono

ballena

león

foca

crab

elephant

whale

monkey

seal

lion

Animales

perros
- son buenas mascotas
- están emparentados con los lobos
- pueden ser de muchos colores

perros y leones
- tienen 2 ojos
- tienen pelo
- tienen 4 patas

leones
- se pueden encontrar en el zoológico
- son animales salvajes

Animals

dogs

- make good house pets
- are related to wolves
- can be many colors

dogs and lions

- have 2 eyes
- have fur
- have 4 legs

lions

- can be found in zoos
- are wild animals

Animales

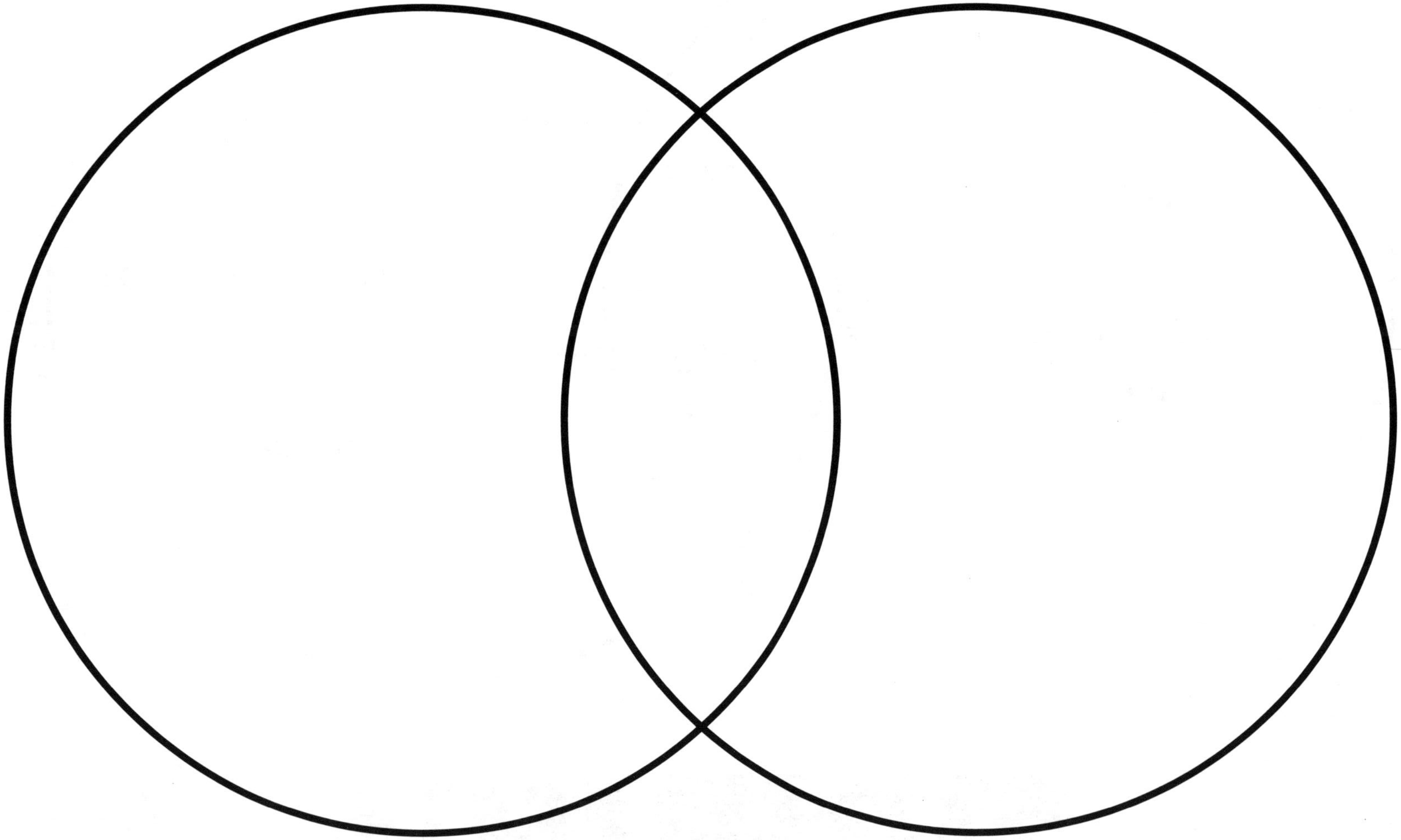

Animals

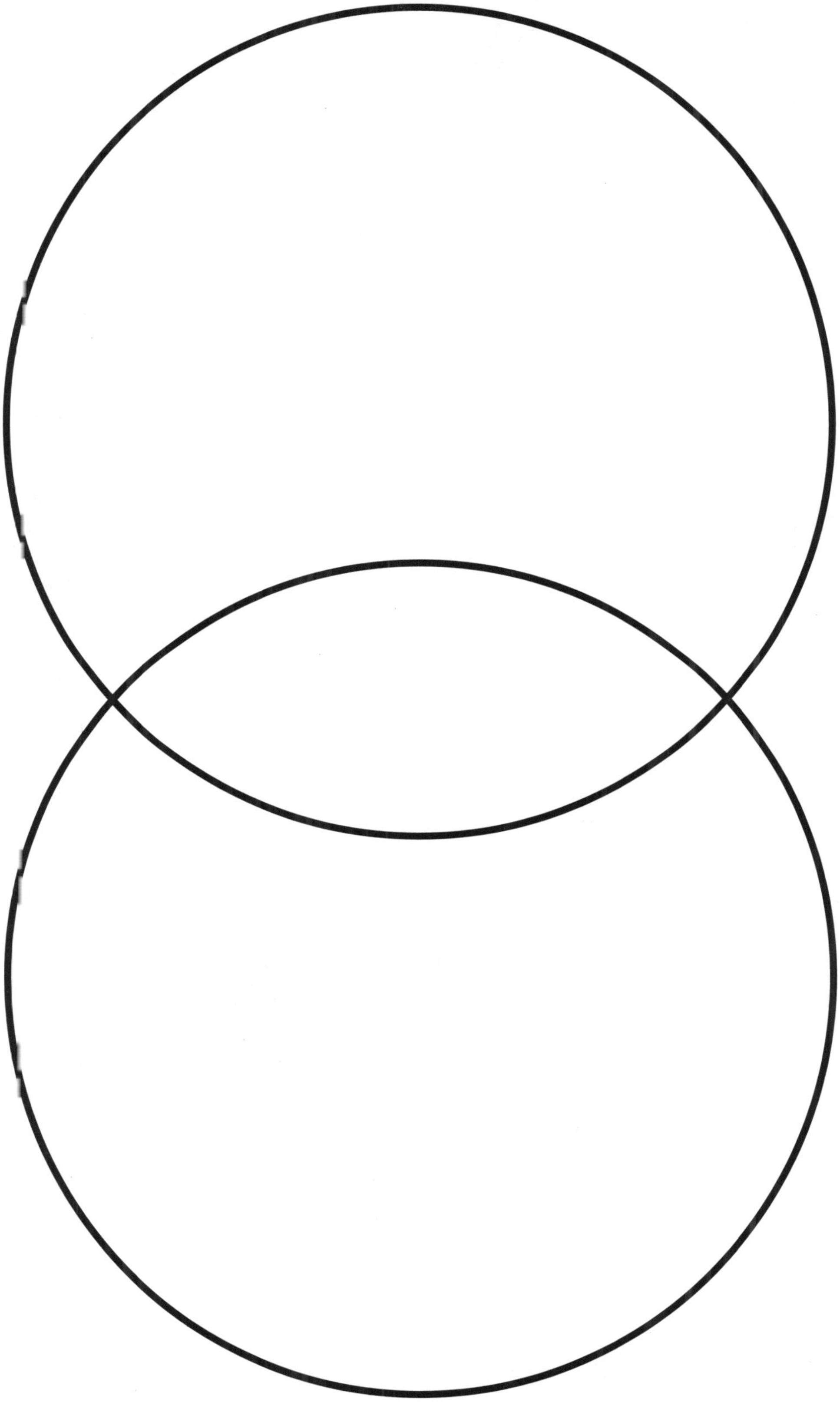

Yo conozco a los animales

Este libro fue hecho por:

Nombre:______________________

I Know About Animals

This Book Was
Created By:

Name: ____________________

cangrejo

ballena

crab

whale

foca

elefante

seal

elephant

mono

león

monkey

lion

gallina

vaca

chicken

cow

caballo

pájaro

horse

bird

perro

gato

dog

cat

Nombre: ____________________________

Haz un círculo alrededor de los animales marinos.

¿Cuántos círculos hiciste? ______

Name: ______________________________

Circle all of the sea animals.

How many sea animals did you circle? ________

Nombre: ______________________________

Haz un círculo alrededor de las mascotas.

¿Cuántos círculos hiciste? ________

Name: ______________________________

Circle all of the pets.

How many pets did you circle? __________

Nombre: ______________________________

Haz un círculo alrededor de los animales del zoológico.

¿Cuántos círculos hiciste? __________

Name: ______________________________

Circle all of the zoo animals.

How many zoo animals did you circle? ________

Nombre: ______________________________

Haz un círculo alrededor de los animales de la granja.

¿Cuántos círculos hiciste? ______

Name: ______________________________

Circle all of the farm animals.

How many farm animals did you circle? ________

Nombre: ______________________

Nombres de los animales

Traza una línea desde el nombre hasta el dibujo correcto.

ballena

gato

mono

pájaro

caballo

león

Name: ______________________________

Animal Match

Draw a line from the word to the correct picture.

whale

cat

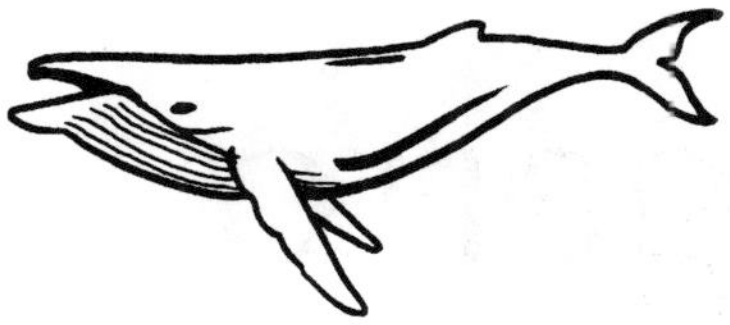

monkey

bird

horse

lion

Nombre: ________________________________

Nombres de los animales

Traza una línea desde el nombre hasta el dibujo correcto.

elefante

perro

gallina

vaca

foca

cangrejo

Name: ______________________________

Animal Match

Draw a line from the word to the correct picture.

elephant

dog

chicken

cow

seal

crab

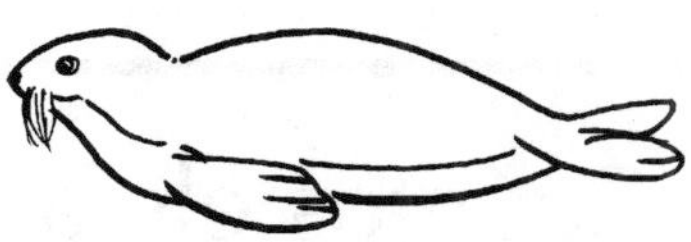

Nombre: ______________________________

Cuenta los animales

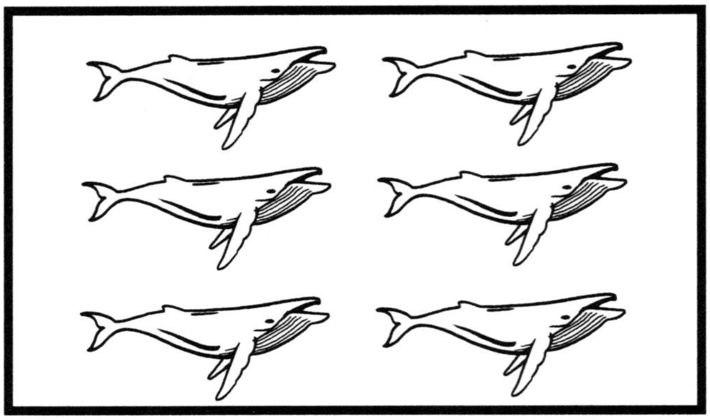

¿Cuántas ballenas? ______

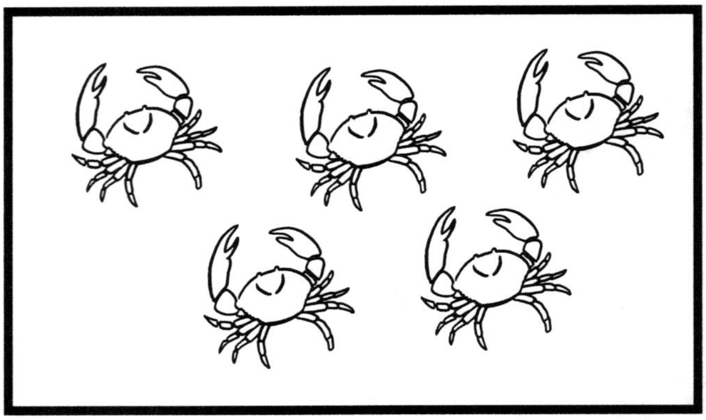

¿Cuántos cangrejos? ______

¿Cuántos leones? ______

¿Cuántos caballos? ______

¿Cuántos elefantes? ______

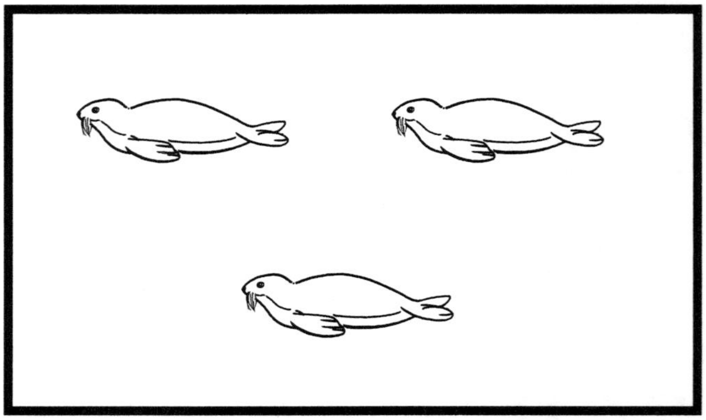

¿Cuántas focas? ______

Name: ______________________________

Count the Animals

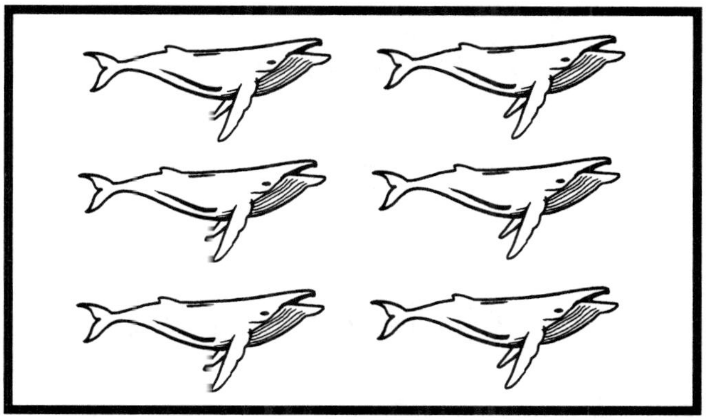

How many whales? _____

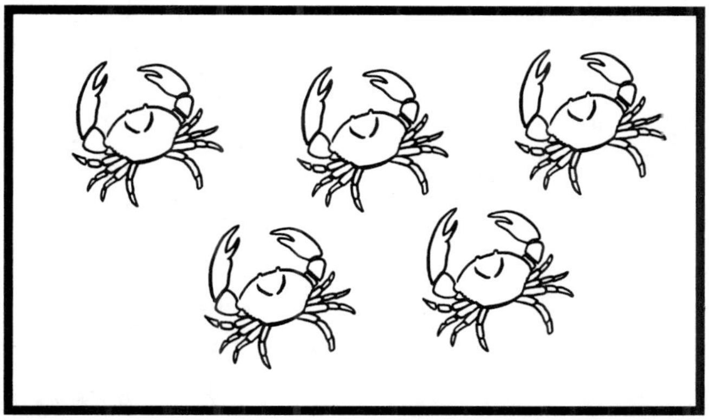

How many crabs? ______

How many lions? _____

How many horses? ______

How many elephants? ______

How many seals? ______

Nombre: ______________________________

Cuenta los animales

Escribe el número en letras.

¿Cuántos perros?

____

¿Cuántos leones?

____

¿Cuántos elefantes?

____

¿Cuántas gallinas?

____

¿Cuántos cangrejos?

____

¿Cuántos monos?

____

Name: ______________________________

Animal Count

Write the number word.

How many dogs?

____

How many lions?

____

How many elephants?

____

How many chickens?

____

How many crabs?

____

How many monkeys?

____

Nombre: ______________________________

Problemas de matemáticas

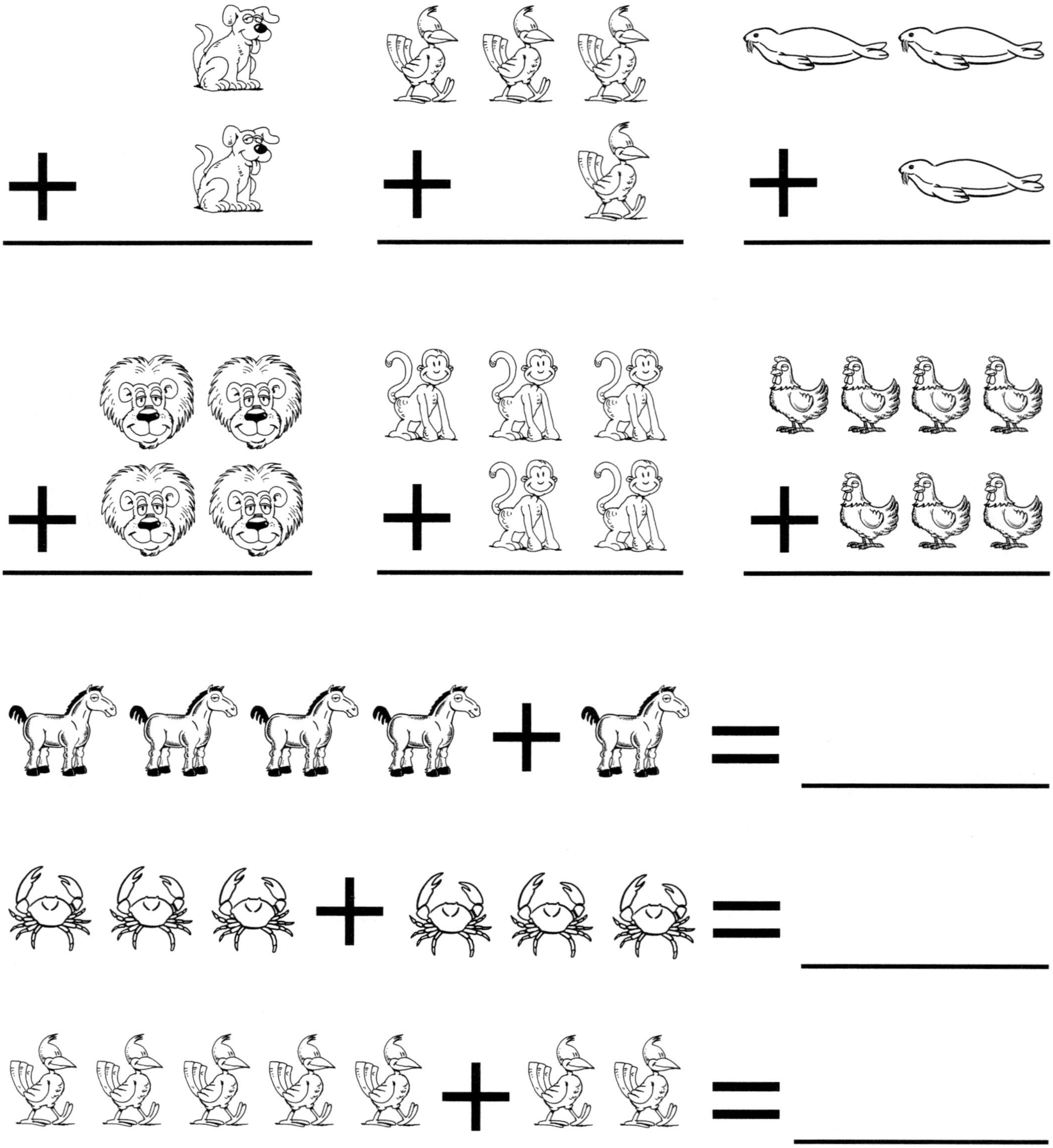

Name: ______________________

Animal Addition

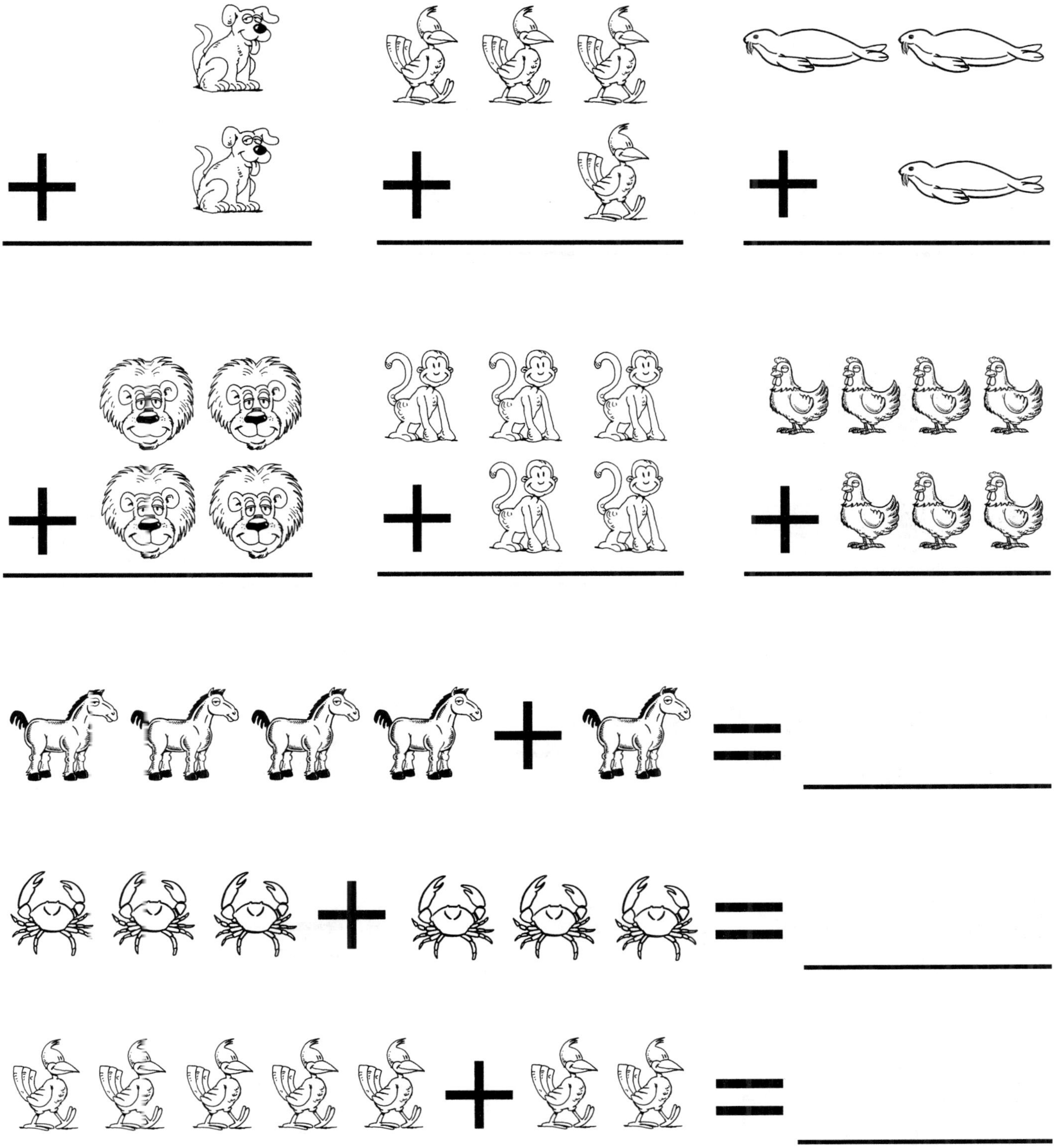

Nombre: ______________________

Problemas de matemáticas

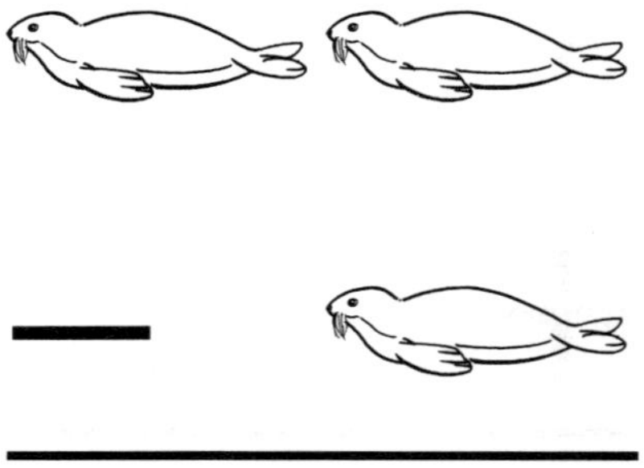

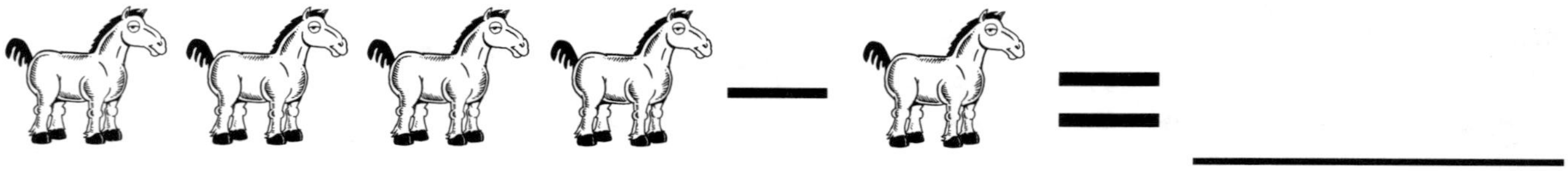

Name: ______________________________

Animal Subtraction

−
______

−
______

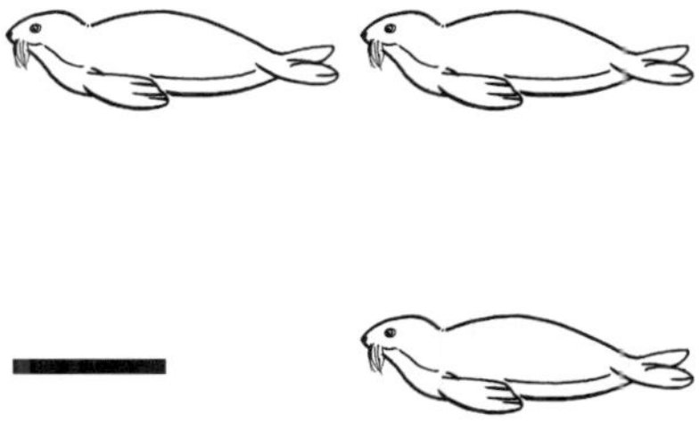
−
______

−
______

−
______

−
______

 = ______

 = ______

 = ______

Nombre: ______________________

Deletrea los nombres de los animales

Escribe el nombre de cada animal.

Name: ______________________________

Animal Spell

Write the name of each animal.

______________ ______________ ______________

______________ ______________ ______________

Nombre: ______________________________

Deletrea los nombres de los animales

Escribe el nombre de cada animal.

__________ __________ __________

__________ __________ __________

Name: ________________________

Animal Spell

Write the name of each animal.

______________ ______________ ______________

______________ ______________ ______________

Nombre: ____________________________

Llena los espacios

Escribe la letra que falta en cada palabra.

___angrejo

___ájaro

___ato

___eón

___aballo

___allina

___ono

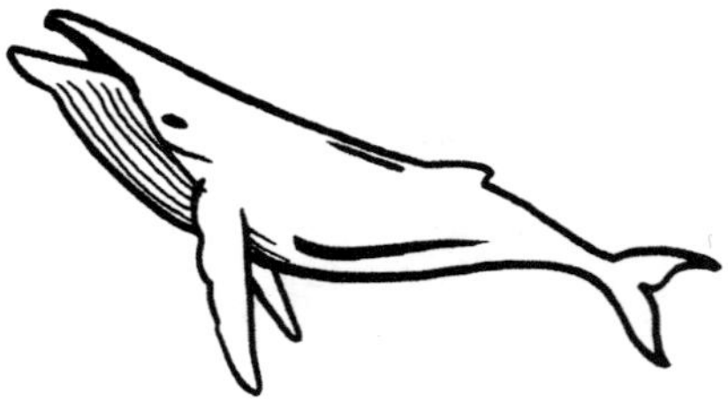

___lefante

___allena

___erro

Name: ______________________________

Fill in the Blanks

Fill in the missing letter in each word.

___rab

___ird

___at

___ion

___orse

___hicken

___onkey

___lephant

___hale

___og

Nombre: ______________________________

Los animales de la granja

Lee el párrafo. Responde a las preguntas. Colorea el dibujo.

Los animales de la granja son animales domésticos que ayudan a los humanos. Proveen alimento o nos ayudan a trabajar. Los pollos y las vacas son animales de la granja que nos proveen alimentos. Los caballos son animales de la granja que nos ayudan con el trabajo. Los animales de la granja no viven dentro de la casa. Ellos nos necesitan para que les demos comida y cobijo.

1. Escribe los nombres de todos animales de la granja que se te ocurran. ______________________________________

   ____

2. Haz un círculo alrededor de los animales de la granja.

mono	caballo	elefante
vaca	gallina	león

3. ¿Cuántos sustantivos hay en el párrafo anterior? ________

4. Los animales de la granja nos dan alimentos como

   ________________. (Haz un círculo alrededor de uno.)

   caramelos y chicle leche y huevos

Name: ______________________________

Farm Animals

Read the story below. Answer the questions. Color the picture.

Farm animals are domestic animals that help people. They provide food or help us do work. We get food from farm animals like chickens and cows. Horses are farm animals that help us with our work. Farm animals do not live in our homes. They need us to provide them with food and shelter.

1. Write the names of all the farm animals you can think of.

____

____

2. Circle the farm animals.

monkey	horse	elephant
cow	chicken	lion

3. How many nouns are in the paragraph above? ________

4. Farm animals provide us with food such as ______________. (Circle one.)

candy and gum   milk and eggs

Nombre: ______________________________

Animales del zoológico

Lee el párrafo. Responde a las preguntas. Colorea el dibujo.

Muchos animales se pueden ver en los zoológicos. Vienen de diferentes lugares del mundo. Algunos de estos animales se consideran animales salvajes en la naturaleza. Los animales del zoológico son importantes porque nos ayudan a conocerlos y así podemos ayudarlos a sobrevivir en su estado natural.

1. Haz un círculo alrededor de los animales que se pueden ver en el zoológico.

   mono perro elefante león

2. Los animales del zoológico nos ayudan a conocerlos y así ayudarlos a sobrevivir en su estado ______________.
3. ¿Cuántas veces se puede encontrar la palabra "zoológico" o "zoológicos" en el párrafo anterior? _______
4. ¿Cuántos sustantivos hay en el párrafo anterior? _______
5. ¿Cuántas palabras de tres letras hay en el párrafo anterior?

   ____

BONO: Escribe el nombre de tu animal favorito del zoológico. ____________________________

Name: ______________________________

Zoo Animals

Read the story below. Answer the questions. Color the picture.

Many animals can be seen in the zoo. They come from different places around the world. Some are considered wild animals in their natural habitats. Zoo animals are important. By observing them, we can learn to help many kinds of animals survive in their natural environments.

1. Circle the animals you might see at a zoo.

   monkey   dog   elephant   lion

2. Zoo animals help us learn how to help animals in their natural ____________________.
3. How many times is the word "zoo" found in the paragraph above? ______
4. How many nouns are in the paragraph above? ______
5. How many three letter words are in the paragraph above?

   ______

BONUS: Write the name of your favorite zoo animal.

____

Nombre: ______________________________

Animales marinos

Lee el párrafo. Responde a las preguntas. Colorea el dibujo.

Los océanos son el hogar de muchos tipos de animales. Algunos viven sólo en el mar, como los peces y las ballenas. Otros tipos de animales marinos viven en los océanos o en las playas, como los cangrejos. Hay miles de animales marinos. Algunos tipos comunes son las ballenas, cangrejos, tiburones y delfines.

1. Hay muchos tipos de animales que viven en el mar.
   (Haz un círculo.) cierto falso
2. Los animales marinos pueden vivir en el agua o en la playa o en ambos medios.
   (Haz un círculo.) cierto falso
3. Hay ________ tipos de animales marinos.
   (Haz un círculo.) dos o tres miles de
4. Nombra un animal marino común. ____________________

BONO:

- Subraya la primera palabra en cada oración del párrafo anterior.
- Haz un círculo alrededor de cada punto en el párrafo anterior.

Name: ______________________________

Sea Animals

Read the story below. Answer the questions. Color the picture.

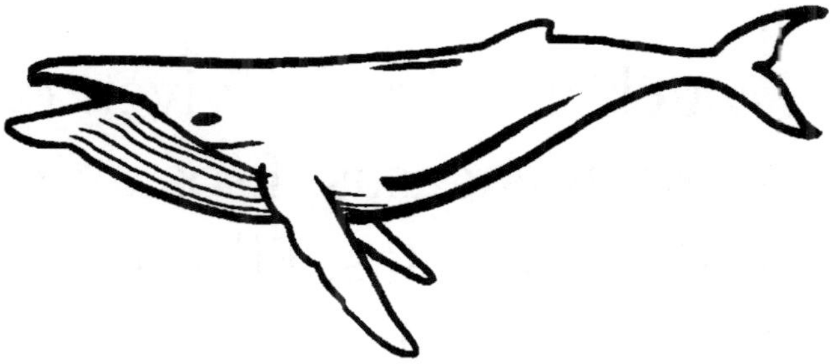

The ocean is the home of many types of animals. Some of the animals live only in the sea, like fish and whales. Other kinds of sea animals live in the ocean part of the time. Sometimes sea animals, like crabs, can be found on beaches. There are thousands of types of sea animals. Some common sea animals are whales, crabs, sharks, and dolphins.

1. Many types of animals live in the sea.
   (Circle one.) true false
2. Sea animals can live in the water, on land, or both.
   (Circle one.) true false
3. There are _______ types of sea animals.
   (Circle one.) two or three thousands of
4. Write the name of a common sea animal.

   ____

BONUS:

- Underline the first word in each sentence in the paragraph above.
- Circle all of the periods in the paragraph above.

Nombre: ______________________________

Mascotas

Lee el párrafo. Responde a las preguntas. Colorea el dibujo.

Muchos animales viven con nosotros en nuestras casas. Esos animales se llaman mascotas. Ellos dependen de nosotros para la comida, agua y amistad. Esos animales se llaman animales domésticos. Algunos animales se pueden entrenar a que nos obedezcan y hagan gracias. Es muy importante que cuidemos bien a nuestras mascotas, pues dependen de nosotros para sus necesidades.

1. Haz un círculo alrededor de las mascotas.

perro	mono	león	vaca
gato	ballena	pájaro	foca

2. Las mascotas dependen de nosotros para ________.

   (Haz un círculo.)

   la comida y el agua   instrucciones de baile

3. ¿Conoces una mascota? Escribe el tipo de animal y el nombre. ______________________________

Name: ______________________________

Pets

Read the story below. Answer the questions. Color the picture.

Many animals live with us in our homes. These animals are called pets. They depend on us for food, water, and companionship. These animals are called domesticated animals. Some animals can be trained to obey us and do tricks! It is important to take good care of our pets because they depend on us to give them what they need.

1. Circle all of the pets.

dog	monkey	lion	cow
cat	whale	bird	seal

2. Pets depend on us for __________. (Circle one.)

   food and water   dancing lessons

3. Do you know a pet? Write what kind of animal it is and its name. ______________________________

Answer Key

Pages 46–47
7 animales marinos/sea animals (3 cangrejos/crabs, 2 ballenas/whales, 2 focas/seals)

Pages 48–49
7 mascotas/pets (3 perros/dogs, 2 gatos/cats, 2 pájaros/birds)

Pages 50–51
6 animales del zoológico/zoo animals (2 leones/lions, 2 elefantes/elephants, 2 monos/monkeys)

Pages 52–53
5 animales de la granja/farm animals (2 gallinas/chickens, 2 caballos/horses, 1 vaca/cow)

Page 54

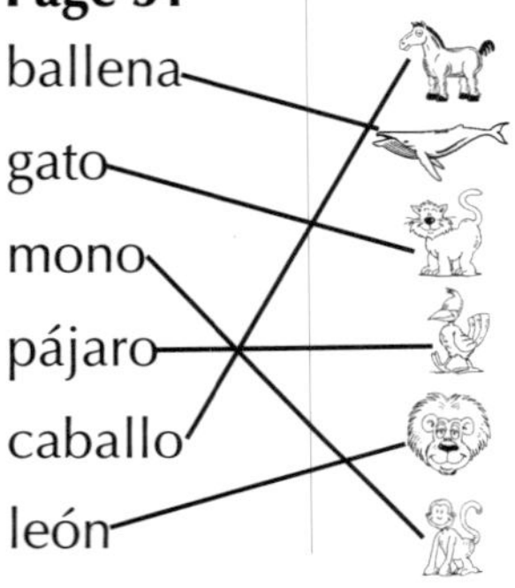

Page 55

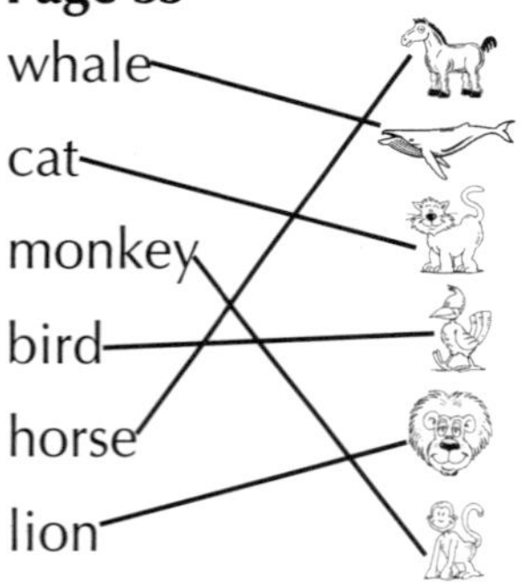

Page 56

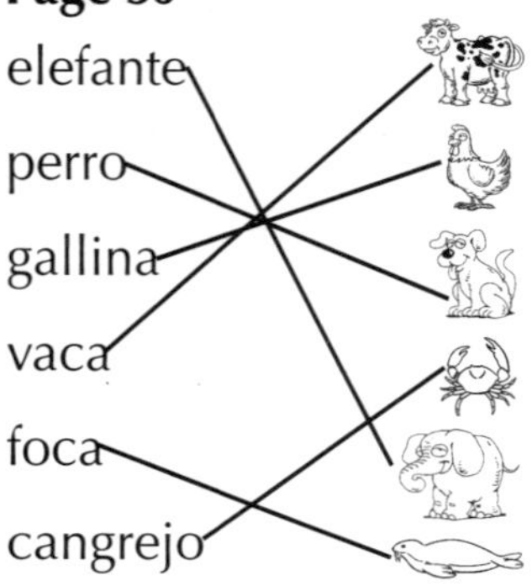

Page 57

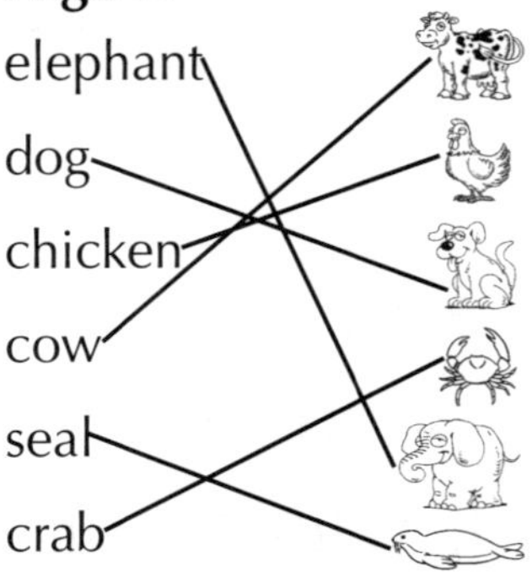

Pages 58–59
From left to right and top to bottom: 6, 5, 8, 4, 7, 3

Page 60
dos, tres, uno, cuatro, dos, tres

Page 61
two, three, one, four, two, three

Pages 62–63
from left to right and top to bottom: 2, 4, 3, 4, 5, 7, 5, 6, 7

Pages 64–65
from left to right and top to bottom: 0, 2, 1, 0, 1, 1, 3, 0, 3

Page 66
from left to right and top to bottom: pájaro, perro, gato, gallina, vaca, caballo

Page 67
from left to right and top to bottom: bird, dog, cat, chicken, cow, horse

Page 68
from left to right and top to bottom: elefante, mono, león, ballena, cangrejo, foca

Page 69
from left to right and top to bottom: elephant, monkey, lion, whale, crab, seal

Page 70
cangrejo, pájaro, gato, león, caballo, gallina, mono, elefante, ballena, perro

Page 71
crab, bird, cat, lion, horse, chicken, monkey, elephant, whale, dog

Page 72
1. Answers will vary but may include: caballo, vaca, gallina, and cerdo. 2. caballo, vaca, gallina; 3. 18; 4. leche y huevos

Page 73
1. Answers will vary but may include: horse, cow, chicken, and pig. 2. horse, cow, chicken; 3. 16; 4. milk and eggs

Page 74
1. mono, elefante, león;
2. natural; 3. 2; 4. 5; 5. 8
BONO: Answers will vary.

Page 75
1. monkey, elephant, lion;
2. environments; 3. 2; 4. 9; 5. 8;
BONUS: Answers will vary.

Page 76
1. cierto; 2. cierto; 3. miles de;
4. Answers will vary.
BONO: The first word in each sentence should be underlined; five periods should be circled.

Page 77
1. true; 2. true; 3. thousands of;
4. Answers will vary.
BONUS: The first word in each sentence should be circled; six periods should be circled.

Page 78
1. perro, gato, pájaro; 2. la comida y el agua; 3. Answers will vary.

Page 79
1. dog, cat, bird; 2. food and water; 3. Answers will vary.